Making Meaning®

THIRD EDITION

Center for the Collaborative Classroom
1250 53rd Street, Suite 3
Emeryville, CA 94606-2965
(800) 666-7270; fax: (510) 464-3670
collaborativeclassroom.org

ISBN 978-1-61003-707-5

Printed in the United States of America

2 3 4 5 6 7 8 9 10 EBM 24 23 22 21 20 19 18 17 16 15

Making Meaning®

THIRD EDITION

Draw a picture of the balloon man.

How I Pictured
The Snowy Day

Draw a picture of the snowy day.

How I Pictured

What I Wonder

About George Washington

I wonder _____

_____

_____

_____

_____

_____

_____

I wonder _____

_____

_____

_____

_____

_____

_____

What I Wonder

About *The Bumblebee Queen*

Name:

I wonder _____

_____

_____

_____

_____

_____

I wonder _____

_____

_____

_____

_____

_____

How I Pictured

Down the Road

Draw a picture about the part where Mama finds Hetty and Papa sitting in the apple tree.

_____

_____

_____

A Time I Had Trouble Falling Asleep

Name:

Make Connections to
Dinosaur Babies

What I Learned and Wonder
About Blue Whales

I learned _____

_____

_____

_____

_____

_____

_____

I wonder _____

_____

_____

_____

_____

_____

_____

I learned _____

_____

_____

_____

_____

_____

_____

I wonder _____

_____

_____

_____

_____

_____

_____

My Diagram of a Velociraptor

Name:

Draw a picture of a velociraptor and label its parts.

My Diagram of a Velociraptor

Equipment Photo Diagram

from *A Day in the Life of a Garbage Collector*

Name:

Equipment Photo Diagram

Lift

Shovel

Hard hat

Safety vest
Garbage collectors must wear brightly colored safety vests in the truck yard and on the route. People can easily see these bright vests.

Gloves

Garbage can

Recycle bin

I learned _____

_____

_____

_____

Thoughts About My Summer Reading

Name:

What kinds of books and stories do you want to read this summer?

_____

_____

_____

_____

Where do you think you might read your books this summer?

_____

_____

_____

_____

_____

What I Liked About Our Reading Community

Name:

Draw a picture of something you enjoyed about the reading community.

_____

_____

_____

Reading Journal

Reading Journal

Name: _____   Date: _____

Reading Journal

Name: _____ Date: _____

Reading Journal

Name: _____ Date: _____

_____

_____

_____

_____

_____

_____

Name: _____ Date: _____

_____

_____

_____

_____

_____

_____

Reading Journal

Name: _____ Date: _____

_____

_____

_____

_____

_____

Name: _____ Date: _____

_____

_____

_____

_____

_____

Reading Journal

Name: _____   Date: _____

_____

_____

_____

_____

_____

_____

Name: _____   Date: _____

_____

_____

_____

_____

_____

Reading Journal

Name: _____ Date: _____

_____

_____

_____

_____

_____

Name: _____ Date: _____

_____

_____

_____

_____

_____

Reading Journal

Name: _____ Date: _____

_____

_____

_____

_____

_____

_____

Name: _____ Date: _____

_____

_____

_____

_____

_____

_____

Reading Journal

Name: _____ Date: _____

_____

_____

_____

_____

_____

_____

Name: _____ Date: _____

_____

_____

_____

_____

_____

_____

Reading Journal

Name: _____ Date: _____

_____

_____

_____

_____

_____

_____

Name: _____ Date: _____

_____

_____

_____

_____

_____

_____

Reading Journal

Name: _____ Date: _____

_____

_____

_____

_____

_____

_____

Name: _____ Date: _____

_____

_____

_____

_____

_____

_____

Reading Journal

Name: _____ Date: _____

_____

_____

_____

_____

_____

_____

Name: _____ Date: _____

_____

_____

_____

_____

_____

_____

Reading Journal

Name: _____ Date: _____

_____

_____

_____

_____

_____

_____

Name: _____ Date: _____

_____

_____

_____

_____

_____

_____

Reading Journal

Name: _____ Date: _____

_____

_____

_____

_____

_____

_____

Name: _____ Date: _____

_____

_____

_____

_____

_____

_____

Reading Journal

Name: _____ Date: _____

_____

_____

_____

_____

_____

_____

Name: _____ Date: _____

_____

_____

_____

_____

_____

_____

Reading Journal

Name: _____ Date: _____

_____

_____

_____

_____

_____

_____

Name: _____ Date: _____

_____

_____

_____

_____

_____

_____